Learning to love ME

Shanita Rogers

Message from Shanita

If asked to make a list of things you like about yourself
and things you do not like about yourself the list of
do not like for many may be longer. Why is that? Is it insecurity?
Are you hanging onto unhealthy behaviors
or thoughts that need to be surrendered to God?
You'll never be in a perfect state. However, you can see
yourself the way God does. That doesn't mean you will
be void of flaws. It simply means that you
value His workmanship.

Spa days and getaways are great! I love them too! However,
they could be more effective if that love extended to depths of
your being. Loving yourself goes beyond saying things like,
"that's just who I am." There may be something that needs to be
uprooted. What seeds were sewn in your life that now have
strong roots that are choking the life out of you or those around you?
Recognizing and unraveling those roots is a process of learning
to love yourself. Love yourself enough to unlearn negative
thinking, toxic behavior, codependency (we call it being needy),
unforgiveness and emotional addictions. Learning to Love Me
Prayer Journal takes you on a 12 week journey of
recalling, reversing and releasing. I pray
that you experience that and more in the coming weeks.
May you experience a healing that you've never known.

BeYouty

Prayer List

List names, needs or other areas of prayer. Check one box each time you pray. This will help you keep track of completed prayers. You may pray multiple times for the same area.

☐☐
☐☐ _____

☐☐
☐☐ _____

☐☐
☐☐ _____

☐☐
☐☐ _____

☐☐
☐☐ _____

☐☐
☐☐ _____

☐☐
☐☐ _____

☐☐
☐☐ _____

☐☐
☐☐ _____

reflection
WHAT DO YOU SEE WITHIN YOURSELF?

What do you love about you?

Week 1

What unhealthy personal trait or insecurity do you have the greatest challenge detaching from?

_____

_____

How do you believe this trait came to be? This may consist of reaching back to your childhood. Remember the goal is not to blame. However, it is to recall, reverse (turn it around and face it) & release the feeling attached to the issue.

_____

_____

_____

_____

In what way does this challenge show up?

_____

_____

_____

_____

_____

_____

_____

_____

_____

_____

_____

_____

_____

_____

_____

_____

_____

_____

What does God say about this concern in the bible?
Reference scriptures that apply.

_____

_____

_____

_____

_____

_____

_____

_____

_____

_____

_____

_____

_____

_____

_____

_____

_____

_____

_____

_____

_____

_____

How do you plan to release this negative feeling, flaw or imperfection into the hands of God? This will allow you to no longer hold it against yourself. It belongs to God! He will now be able to carry the weight that you have been burdened down with in life. If it is a physical trait, allow God to show you your beauty regardless of the imperfection.

Pray for the release.

_____

_____

_____

_____

_____

_____

_____

_____

_____

_____

_____

_____

_____

Week 2

What unhealthy personal trait or insecurity do you have the greatest challenge detaching from?

_____

_____

How do you believe this issue came to be? This may consist of reaching back to your childhood. Remember the goal is not to blame. However, it is to recall, reverse (turn it around & face it) & release the imperfection.

_____

_____

_____

_____

In what way does this challenge show up?

What does God says about this concern in the bible?
Reference scriptures that apply.

_____

_____

_____

_____

_____

_____

_____

_____

_____

_____

_____

_____

_____

_____

_____

_____

_____

_____

_____

_____

_____

How do you plan to release this negative feeling, flaw or imperfection into the hands of God? This will allow you to no longer hold it against yourself. It belongs to God! He will now be able to carry the weight that you have been burdened down with in life. If it is a physical trait, allow God to show you your beauty regardless of the imperfection.
Pray for the release.

_____

_____

_____

_____

_____

_____

_____

_____

_____

_____

_____

_____

Week 3

What unhealthy personal trait or insecurity do you have the greatest challenge detaching from?

_____

_____

How do you believe this trait came to be? This may consist of reaching back to your childhood. Remember the goal is not to blame. However, it is to recall, reverse (turn it around and face it) & release the feeling attached to the issue.

_____

_____

_____

_____

In what way does this challenge show up?

_____

_____

_____

_____

_____

_____

_____

_____

_____

_____

_____

_____

_____

_____

_____

_____

_____

_____

What does God says about this concern in the bible?
Reference scriptures that apply.

_____

_____

_____

_____

_____

_____

_____

_____

_____

_____

_____

_____

_____

_____

_____

_____

_____

_____

How do you plan to release this negative feeling, flaw or imperfection into the hands of God? This will allow you to no longer hold it against yourself. It belongs to God! He will now be able to carry the weight that you have been burdened down with in life. If it is a physical trait, allow God to show you your beauty regardless of the imperfection.

Pray for a release.

_____

_____

_____

_____

_____

_____

_____

_____

_____

_____

_____

_____

_____

Week 4

What unhealthy personal trait or insecurity do you have the greatest challenge detaching from?

_____

_____

How do you believe this trait came to be? This may consist of reaching back to your childhood. Remember the goal is not to blame. However, it is to recall, reverse (turn it around and face it) & release the feeling attached to the issue.

_____

_____

_____

_____

In what way does this challenge show up?

_____

_____

_____

_____

_____

_____

_____

_____

_____

_____

_____

_____

_____

_____

_____

_____

_____

_____

_____

_____

_____

What does God says about this concern in the bible?
Reference scriptures that apply.

_____

_____

_____

_____

_____

_____

_____

_____

_____

_____

_____

_____

_____

_____

_____

_____

_____

_____

_____

How do you plan to release this negative feeling, flaw or imperfection into the hands of God? This will allow you to no longer hold it against yourself. It belongs to God! He will now be able to carry the weight that you have been burdened down with in life. If it is a physical trait, allow God to show you your beauty regardless of the imperfection.

Pray for a release.

_____

_____

_____

_____

_____

_____

_____

_____

_____

_____

_____

_____

Week 5

What unhealthy personal trait or insecurity do you have the greatest challenge detaching from?

_____

_____

How do you believe this trait came to be? This may consist of reaching back to your childhood. Remember the goal is not to blame. However, it is to recall, reverse (turn it around and face it) & release the feeling attached to the issue.

_____

_____

_____

_____

In what way does this challenge show up?

_____

_____

_____

_____

_____

_____

_____

_____

_____

_____

_____

_____

_____

_____

_____

_____

_____

_____

_____

What does God says about this concern in the bible?
Reference scriptures that apply.

_____

_____

_____

_____

_____

_____

_____

_____

_____

_____

_____

_____

_____

_____

_____

_____

_____

_____

How do you plan to release this negative feeling, flaw or imperfection into the hands of God? This will allow you to no longer hold it against yourself. It belongs to God! He will now be able to carry the weight that you have been burdened down with in life. If it is a physical trait, allow God to show you your beauty regardless of the imperfection.

Pray for a release.

_____

_____

_____

_____

_____

_____

_____

_____

_____

_____

_____

_____

Week 6

What unhealthy personal trait or insecurity do you have the greatest challenge detaching from?

_____

_____

How do you believe this trait came to be? This may consist of reaching back to your childhood. Remember the goal is not to blame. However, it is to recall, reverse (turn it around and face it) & release the feeling attached to the issue.

_____

_____

_____

_____

In what way does this challenge show up?

_____

_____

_____

_____

_____

_____

_____

_____

_____

_____

_____

_____

_____

_____

_____

_____

_____

_____

_____

What does God says about this concern in the bible?
Reference scriptures that apply.

_____

_____

_____

_____

_____

_____

_____

_____

_____

_____

_____

_____

_____

_____

_____

_____

_____

_____

How do you plan to release this negative feeling, flaw or imperfection into the hands of God? This will allow you to no longer hold it against yourself. It belongs to God! He will now be able to carry the weight that you have been burdened down with in life. If it is a physical trait, allow God to show you your beauty regardless of the imperfection.

Pray for a release.

_____

_____

_____

_____

_____

_____

_____

_____

_____

_____

_____

_____

_____

_____

Week 7

What unhealthy personal trait or insecurity do you have the greatest challenge detaching from?

_____

_____

How do you believe this trait came to be? This may consist of reaching back to your childhood. Remember the goal is not to blame. However, it is to recall, reverse (turn it around and face it) & release the feeling attached to the issue.

_____

_____

_____

_____

In what way does this challenge show up?

What does God says about this concern in the bible?
Reference scriptures that apply.

_____

_____

_____

_____

_____

_____

_____

_____

_____

_____

_____

_____

_____

_____

_____

_____

_____

_____

_____

How do you plan to release this negative feeling, flaw or imperfection into the hands of God? This will allow you to no longer hold it against yourself. It belongs to God! He will now be able to carry the weight that you have been burdened down with in life. If it is a physical trait, allow God to show you your beauty regardless of the imperfection.
Pray for a release.

_____

_____

_____

_____

_____

_____

_____

_____

_____

_____

Week 8

What unhealthy personal trait or insecurity do you have the greatest challenge detaching from?

_____

_____

How do you believe this trait came to be? This may consist of reaching back to your childhood. Remember the goal is not to blame. However, it is to recall, reverse (turn it around and face it) & release the feeling attached to the issue.

_____

_____

_____

_____

In what way does this challenge show up?

What does God says about this concern in the bible?
Reference scriptures that apply.

_____

_____

_____

_____

_____

_____

_____

_____

_____

_____

_____

_____

_____

_____

_____

_____

_____

_____

_____

How do you plan to release this negative feeling, flaw or imperfection into the hands of God? This will allow you to no longer hold it against yourself. It belongs to God! He will now be able to carry the weight that you have been burdened down with in life. If it is a physical trait, allow God to show you your beauty regardless of the imperfection.

Pray for a release..

_____

_____

_____

_____

_____

_____

_____

_____

_____

_____

_____

Week 9

What unhealthy personal trait or insecurity do you have the greatest challenge detaching from?

_____

_____

How do you believe this trait came to be? This may consist of reaching back to your childhood. Remember the goal is not to blame. However, it is to recall, reverse (turn it around and face it) & release the feeling attached to the issue.

_____

_____

_____

_____

In what way does this challenge show up?

What does God says about this concern in the bible?
Reference scriptures that apply.

_____

_____

_____

_____

_____

_____

_____

_____

_____

_____

_____

_____

_____

_____

_____

_____

_____

_____

_____

_____

How do you plan to release this negative feeling, flaw or imperfection into the hands of God? This will allow you to no longer hold it against yourself. It belongs to God! He will now be able to carry the weight that you have been burdened down with in life. If it is a physical trait, allow God to show you your beauty regardless of the imperfection.

Pray for a release.

_____

_____

_____

_____

_____

_____

_____

_____

_____

_____

_____

_____

Week 10

What unhealthy personal trait or insecurity do you have the greatest challenge detaching from?

_____

_____

How do you believe this trait came to be? This may consist of reaching back to your childhood. Remember the goal is not to blame. However, it is to recall, reverse (turn it around and face it) & release the feeling attached to the issue.

_____

_____

_____

_____

In what way does this challenge show up?

What does God says about this concern in the bible?
Reference scriptures that apply.

_____

_____

_____

_____

_____

_____

_____

_____

_____

_____

_____

_____

_____

_____

_____

_____

_____

_____

_____

How do you plan to release this negative feeling, flaw or imperfection into the hands of God? This will allow you to no longer hold it against yourself. It belongs to God! He will now be able to carry the weight that you have been burdened down with in life. If it is a physical trait, allow God to show you your beauty regardless of the imperfection.
Pray for a release.

_____

_____

_____

_____

_____

_____

_____

_____

_____

_____

_____

_____

Week 11

What unhealthy personal trait or insecurity do you have the greatest challenge detaching from?

_____

_____

How do you believe this trait came to be? This may consist of reaching back to your childhood. Remember the goal is not to blame. However, it is to recall, reverse (turn it around and face it) & release the feeling attached to the issue.

_____

_____

_____

_____

In what way does this challenge show up?

What does God says about this concern in the bible?
Reference scriptures that apply.

_____

_____

_____

_____

_____

_____

_____

_____

_____

_____

_____

_____

_____

_____

_____

_____

_____

_____

How do you plan to release this negative feeling, flaw or imperfection into the hands of God? This will allow you to no longer hold it against yourself. It belongs to God! He will now be able to carry the weight that you have been burdened down with in life. If it is a physical trait, allow God to show you your beauty regardless of the imperfection.

Pray for a release.

_____

_____

_____

_____

_____

_____

_____

_____

_____

_____

_____

Week 12

What unhealthy personal trait or insecurity do you have the greatest challenge detaching from?

_____

_____

How do you believe this trait came to be? This may consist of reaching back to your childhood. Remember the goal is not to blame. However, it is to recall, reverse (turn it around and face it) & release the feeling attached to the issue.

_____

_____

_____

_____

In what way does this challenge show up?

How do you plan to release this negative feeling, flaw or imperfection into the hands of God? This will allow you to no longer hold it against yourself. It belongs to God! He will now be able to carry the weight that you have been burdened down with in life. If it is a physical trait, allow God to show you your beauty regardless of the imperfection.
Pray for a release.

_____

_____

_____

_____

_____

_____

_____

_____

_____

_____

_____

_____

Answered Prayers

_____

_____

_____

_____

_____

_____

_____

_____

_____

_____

_____

_____

Prayer

I pray for a heart to accept and love who
you have created me to be.
As I seek your word unveil my identity. When I feel weak let your
strength extend reach to my mind.
Remove any intent or constant urge to focus on shortcomings.
I will rely on You for confidence and security.
You are my strong tower and safe place.
Thank you God for healing a heart of brokenness. Thank you for
being my covering, comfort & protection in my toughest hour.
I pray for forward moving thinking.
I believe you for the ability to encourage myself and stand on your promises.
As your daughter I trust that your word will never return void.
I praise you for all of these things in Jesus' name.
Amen

Affirmation

I give myself permission to cry when needed but smile often.
I will be present when I can and not beat myself up when I cannot.
I will not push myself to be superwoman instead be a woman who is super.
I understand that I cannot be all things to everyone to keep
peace yet lack my own.
I cannot be everywhere at once leaving scattered pieces of me and
lacking sanity when I arrive home. I cannot control if others receive
my boundaries as a no to them. It is a yes to me and I accept it.
I will prioritize my life in a manner that allows me to live well.
I will not live in my past even if others know it.
I see my future as God does.
I am me. There is only one me. I must take care of me.
I must be filled to have the ability to pour into anyone else.
If I am empty there is nothing left to give.
I rely on God to replenish wells that have run dry, mend those broken
pieces and strengthen me when weak. I see myself as God does.

To book Shanita for a speaking engagement email realrawandrighteous@gmail.com.

Follow Shanita on social media @RealRawRighteous. You may also purchase her book "Beauty Beneath the Surface" on major e-commerce websites.

Made in the USA
Columbia, SC
08 June 2021